Welcome...

... to A Sea Fishing Year!

After the complete success of our first bookazine in 2011, which we completely sold out of, we felt compelled to produce another – only this time with a slightly different flavour...

When you're unable to get out fishing, for whatever reason, and you then find yourself relaxing in your favourite chair, don't put the television on – why not indulge yourself by enjoying a really good read about your favourite pastime? But what's that I hear, you've nothing new to read? Well here it is – A Sea Fishing Year! This information-packed publication will provide you with your sea fishing 'fix' on those occasions when you're just not able to hit the beach or board a boat.

Our fishing has traditionally been seasonal and, to this end, we have assembled this second fabulous publication to take you through the entire year – season by season – with the best features on our favourite species. It includes feature-length, action-packed stories, along with plenty of 'how to' information too – so there's definitely something you can get your teeth into. Whether you're a novice or an expert, you'll find all you need to know about targeting particular species, both from the shore and boat, at specific times of the year, then you can experience a 'live' story relating events as we put theory into practice!

Not only will you satisfy your sea fishing cravings, you'll also be better armed and loaded with the information you need to tackle your next excursion. So, put the kettle on, throw the TV remote away and enjoy this action-packed bookazine.

Let's go sea fishing together once again!

Barney

Barney Wright,
Editor, Total Sea Fishing

CONTENTS

A Sea Fishing Year.

Published by David Hall Publishing Ltd. The advertisements and editorial content of this publication are the copyright of David Hall Publishing Ltd and may not be quoted, copied or reproduced without prior permission of the publisher.

Copyright © 2012 - Edited by Barney Wright - Designed by John Cauchi - Reprographics by Derek Mooney and Adam Mason - Sub edited by Dean Kirkman

Big cod move closer to the shore under the protection of darkness.

Make Your Next Cod A
MONSTER

Cod are the main target species through the winter months and our top tips and advice on bait, rigs and venues will help you bag more fish!

Cod are greedy, fast-growing fish that will eat just about anything they come across, including worms, crustaceans, brittle stars, herring, sprats, sandeels and squid. Larger cod tend to feed more on fish because they're protein packed and help the cod to grow. Cod have even been known to swallow white plastic drinking cups! While cod may occasionally take a single worm or small bait, with their huge appetites and mouths to match it's best to use big baits to achieve the best results. Big baits also put a better scent trail in the water for the fish to follow and will last longer.

REELS AND LINE

For fishing over clean ground, a 6500-sized multiplier or 7000 to 8000-sized fixed-spool reel loaded with 12lb to 18lb line is all you need. Monofilament is best on multipliers but fixed-spool users can gain distance by using braided lines as they're much thinner than mono of the same breaking strain. If casting from a beach, always use a shockleader with the rule of 10lb of breaking strain for every ounce you're casting, so a 6oz lead will need a minimum 60lb shockleader for safety. Tactics for rough ground are different because casting distance isn't as crucial as it is on a shallow, sandy beach. Fast-retrieve multipliers in the 7000 size or a Daiwa SL30 or SL40 loaded with 30lb to 40lb line will be needed to cope with abrasion and heavy hauling.

BAITS

The most common and most effective baits are lug, squid and crab, either on their own or in a cocktail of two or all three. White rag constitutes a must-have bait for the match angler; a lug bait tipped with white rag can make the difference between a few fish or nothing. Whites are difficult to find and dig and very expensive if you can find somewhere that actually sells them. A whole squid can be a very effective bait for big fish but, due to their size and shape, they're difficult to cast far. Other baits that work well in some local areas are blueys, mussels, razorfish and clams.

If you can fish deep, clear water, pirks and soft-plastic lures are a sporting way to catch cod.

Livebaits are a very good tactic for sorting out the bigger fish; the rig will have a small hook baited with worm to tempt a small pout or whiting next to a big hook to catch the cod. This method calls for a lot of patience but uses very little bait; all you have to do is cast the rig out and wait until you see the rod tip rattle as a pout takes the worm. Ignore the little bites and leave the little fish out there until Mr Cod finds it, then you'll see the rod tip slam over – make sure you have the drag backed off, otherwise your rod could be dragged in.

RODS

Cod inhabit and feed over many different types of ground, from shallow sand and shingle beaches to deep-water rock marks, so choose the right gear for the job. For clean ground, regular beachcasters that will cast 4oz to 6oz are fine but shallow beaches may need long casts of 100 metres or more on calm days. Fishing rough ground requires a more powerful rod with a stiffer tip to haul your rig and fish out of the gullies and kelp. When you get a bite you need to wind down, lowering the tip, then lift sharply and keep winding to keep your gear and fish above the snags.

RIGS

One of the best rigs for cod over clean ground is a clipped-down rig, either with a single hook or Pennel-rigged hooks. Because the clipped-down bait is streamlined, it'll cast further and protect the bait when it hits the sea. Pulley rigs are best for rough-ground codding because the weight of the fish will lift the lead clear of any snags.

HOOKS

It's pretty simple to choose the right hook because big baits and big mouths require big hooks, so sizes 2/0 to 4/0 are good sizes for codling but if you're using big cocktail baits then go for 6/0 to 8/0s; basically match the hook to the size of the bait that you're using. Also, thick-wire hooks can be an advantage because, although cod are big and powerful, they do have fairly soft mouths that can tear if the wire is thin and you pull too hard. Another reason to use good-quality, strong hooks is when you're trying to land a good fish; fine-wire hooks are okay for codling but will straighten out if you're trying to pull a bigger fish through the backwash.

TIME AND TIDE

Local knowledge can make the difference between fish on the beach and a blank session, so do your homework to find out whether the fish feed over the low tide or high tide for best results. Night fishing will usually produce more fish when they move closer to the shore to feed, but in rough, windy conditions when the sea is heavily coloured, good catches can be made during the day. Cod fishing can be best just after a few days of strong onshore winds that have stirred up the sea bed and washed out worms and shellfish, providing an easy feed.

COD FACTS

There are many different species of cod around the world but the three main varieties are the Atlantic cod (*Gadus morhua*), the Greenland cod (*Gadus ogac*) and the Pacific cod (*Gadus macrocephalus*).
The average size caught from the shore is from a few ounces to several pounds but cod into double figures can be caught from several locations around the country. Cod of more than 200lb have been caught by commercial fishermen but are probably things of the past, although 100lb cod are still occasionally caught in northern Norway.

IDENTIFICATION

The cod has three rounded dorsal fins, two anal fins and small pelvic fins. Its upper jaw extends over its lower jaw, with its obvious chin barbel. It has a distinct white lateral line running from the gills above the pectoral fin to the base of the tail fin. Our Atlantic cod can be found in two colour variations depending on where they live; there's the usual grey-green and a reddish brown when they live and feed in the kelp over rocky ground.

BREEDING

Cod divide into various stocks and there's little interchange between them, although they may travel 200 miles to their breeding grounds. The different stocks are found in the Arctic/Norwegian region and the North Sea on the eastern side of the Atlantic and Iceland, Greenland, Newfoundland and Labrador in the northern Atlantic.
A large female cod can lay up to five million eggs but only a small number of these will survive predators and overfishing to become adults.
Spawning can take place between January and April way offshore in depths down to 200 metres, in water temperatures between 4°C and 6°C.
The major spawning grounds around the UK are in the mid and southern North Sea, the mouth of the Bristol Channel, the Irish Channel and off northwestern Scotland.

TERRAIN

The best place to find the fish is on or near features. This could be a worm bed, a gulley scoured out by the current or boulders and rough ground. These features will either trap food that is being carried by the current or offer somewhere to hide for shrimps, crabs or little fish. The cod will know this and regularly hunt for food, in a similar way to us knowing where the café is for breakfast.

TOP 10 LOCATIONS

SCOTLAND – NORTH BERWICK HARBOUR, ROCKS AND BEACHES, EAST LOTHIAN

These marks fish best when a big easterly or northeasterly sea is running and double-figure cod are taken most winters. Care needs to be taken on the rock marks in such conditions. Night fishing and flood tides are best but long casting is not required. Weed can be a problem on the beach to the right of the harbour. Travel light to be mobile and pack a stiff rod and tough Saltist 30-type reel with 30lb mono. Rotten-bottom Pennel rigs with 3/0 to 5/0 size hooks baited with lug or squid baits provide the best results.

NORTHEAST – SEAHAM TO BEADNELL

Good fish can come from anywhere along this stretch but it needs a good onshore blow to bring them in. Most fishing is into rough ground so rotten-bottom and pulley rigs are best. The top baits are lug, squid and crab or a cocktails of these.

EAST YORKSHIRE – ALDBROUGH TO SPURN

These beaches are mostly clean with just the odd snag and, while distance casting can pay off here, cod can be caught 30 to 50 metres out if the water is heavily coloured. Night fishing produces the best results but decent catches can be made during the day if there's plenty of colour. As with other marks, the top baits are worm, squid and crab.

SUFFOLK – ALDEBURGH AND ORFORD ISLAND

The beaches offer access to deep water close in so long casting isn't always necessary. As with other venues, a good blow to stir things up brings the fish in and double-figure cod can and have been hooked just 30 metres out. Worm, squid and crab will take codling, with whole squid or livebaits for the big boys.

KENT – DUNGENESS

Dungy is another famous deep-water beach and, while it doesn't produce as well as it did in the old days, it still produces good fish every year. Big bunches of black lug or lug-and-squid cocktails work well here.

DORSET – ABBOTSBURY

Codling turn up at Chesil in the autumn with the biggest fish showing in December and January. Abbotsbury Beach has a reputation for throwing up a few very big cod, especially at the 'Dragons Teeth', a half-mile walk to the left of the car park. Whole squid or lug-and-squid cocktails and livebait tactics work well here. It's very steep here and care should be taken in rough weather because the shingle can be dragged away by the backwash.

CORNWALL – LOOE

This is another very steep beach with deep water close in where care must be taken in rough weather. Night fishing is best but specimen-sized cod can turn up at any time. Long casts are not always necessary due to the depth of water close in. Use big worms, squid and launce for bait.

SOMERSET – SAND POINT

The Bristol Channel experiences some of the biggest tides in the world and these strong currents stir up the silt and sediment so that the water is constantly the colour of gravy. Powerful gear is needed to cope with the currents, the snags and when you hook a lunker. Pulley rigs are favoured here, baited with worm, squid and crab.

SOUTH WALES – REDWICK & OGMORE DEEPS

These marks are on the north side of the Bristol Channel and both have produced good catches of big cod. Once again, choose powerful gear to cope with strong tides, rough ground and the chance of a big fish. The usual baits – worm, crab and squid – will produce.

FYLDE COAST – ROSSALL

Like many other beaches around the country, it's not as productive as it used to be, but rough weather and long casts will produce the best results. Use streamlined rigs baited with local black lug. Other baits to try are crab, squid and mussel.

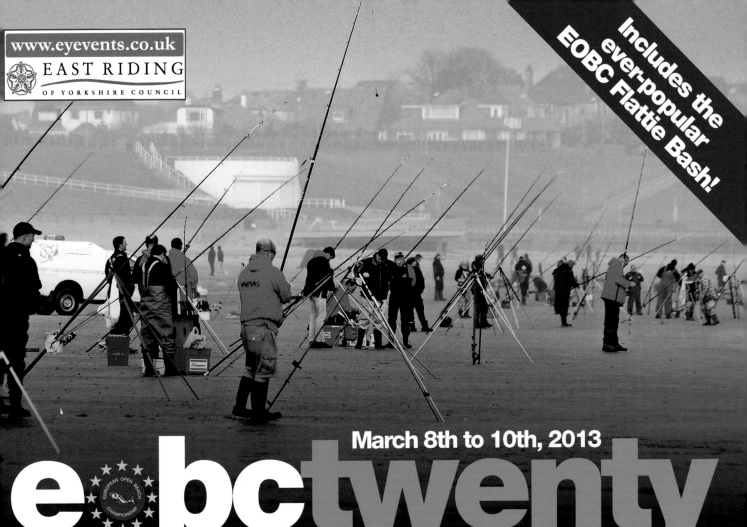

www.eyevents.co.uk
EAST RIDING OF YORKSHIRE COUNCIL

Includes the ever-popular EOBC Flattie Bash!

March 8th to 10th, 2013

e○bctwenty

Make history in the world's biggest sea angling event

europeanopenbeachchampionship

Celebrating its 20th anniversary, the EOBC in East Yorkshire is the biggest three-day beach fishing festival in the world. It attracts shore angling stars from all over the UK and Europe and in 2013 it is offering a prize fund of £35,000[*]!

in association with

Sand le Mere HOLIDAY VILLAGE

Total **Sea** FISHING

Official Travel Partner
P&O Ferries

For news on this year's event and to register for tickets visit:

www.eyevents.co.uk

[*] anticipated prize fund   *Event Information:* **Paul Roggeman**   Tel: **01482 391668**   E-mail: **info@eyevents.co.uk**

Boat Your Best-Ever
WHITING

Whiting can show in plague proportions and we show
you how to target the bigger fish of the shoals.

Every winter the south coast is invaded by swarms of little whiting. This can be great for anglers, as the little critters can often provide a bit of fun for us while we wait for that lunker cod to come along. Although boat-caught whiting are normally much bigger than the aptly named 'pin whiting' that beach anglers happily drag ashore, the whiting can never be thought of as sportfish, and a 4lb fish is a real good 'un!

In the waters around Portsmouth these fish are typically 8oz to 1lb in size, but there are often bigger fish among them that we can specifically target, which is well worth doing because they make lovely eating fish too! Very often these bigger specimens are caught by accident by anglers using bigger baits to target cod.

RECORDS

WHITING (*Merlangius merlangus*)
Boat: 6lb 12oz caught in 1981 by N R Croft out of Falmouth, Cornwall.
Shore: 4lb 0oz 7dr, caught in 1984 by T Dell off Abbotsbury Beach, Dorset.

A big whiting will always bring a smile to an angler's face!

CANNIBALS!

The best baits for regular whiting include most fish baits, such as mackerel, bluey, sandeels, rag and lug. The larger whiting, however, are distinctly cannibalistic and have a real preference for a fresh piece of whiting flesh! That's absolutely ideal for us because, very often, the small whiting are so numerous that they are really easy to catch and offer great free bait. In fact, they aren't the only species of fish that enjoy a fresh piece of whiting – the bass population will be actively hunting whiting as a part of their own seasonal food programme, and cod also eat whiting as a standard part of their diet!

A fresh whiting fillet makes great bait because, being fresh, it's still quite tough and stays on the hook much longer than frozen fish baits. Although it may not appear to be so full of oil and scent as other baits, it does hold plenty of pulling power for the other fish because they are so tuned into the smell of whiting as a food source.

TACTICS

When fishing a flowing trace along the sea bed when the tide is running hard, it's very often beneficial to change to a paternoster rig with baits just off the bottom as the tide slackens. This definitely applies when fishing for whiting.

Over slack water the approach is very simple – any paternoster rig, mackerel feathers, Hokkais and the like will catch whiting, and plenty of them, when baited with a piece of whiting flesh. But for the bigger specimens it's better to use larger rigs such as muppet paternosters. They work so much better for these big fish that are feeding and hunting hard – also, they are competing against the other fish in the shoal, so have less time to really inspect the baits. Instead they rely on the scent as a deciding factor, along with the great visual effect that the muppets have. The larger rigs also work well for cod that attack by sight over slack water and, as they are stronger, will give you a greater chance of getting the bigger fish to the boat!

Luminous beads on the snood attract whiting. Note the sharp teeth!

As the tide runs it's then time to resort to a long flowing trace attached to a weighted boom. Try 40lb clear trace line because it's strong enough to land any stray cod, but is also more resistant to tangling and being ruined by the whiting, because they have a habit of tying the rigs up in knots.

On the flowing trace it's important to use really sharp hooks, because the flesh is quite tough and covered in loads of small scales. Very sharp hooks pull through the pieces of bait much more easily, and when done properly you end up with a decent, tidy bait rather than a bunch of mush, which is so often the result of blunt hooks.

Hook sizes can still be on the small side. Go for a size 1 quality Aberdeen style – a Kamasan B940 is perfect for the job because, as well as being sharp, it is really strong and will handle big fish too!

LUMI BEADS AND MUPPETS

Adding attractors certainly doesn't put the fish off in any way, and whiting do respond to them. Over the years, luminous attractors, in the form of beads and small muppets, have been proven to work really well. They can be added to both paternoster rigs and flowing traces just above the hook. Floating lumi beads not only add the luminescence, but they also add a little buoyancy and movement to the bait, which often proves too much to resist for the feeding fish.

HOW TO PREPARE A FRESH WHITING FOR BAIT

Typically the size of whiting that we use as bait would be 12oz. These fish don't hold a great deal of fillet flesh and are also quite boney. So a really sharp knife is essential to get the best out of one and to cut it up neatly into bait-sized sections. As with blunt hooks, a blunt knife will result in trashy bait, which will, in turn, result in fewer fish caught.

To begin with, the fish needs to be filleted, with the fillet then cut up into bait-sized sections. Each bait should then be threaded neatly along the hook and the top end also pulled up over the hook knot – this will hold it in place. When threaded on properly, these baits will flow nicely on the flowing trace, almost resembling a group of small fish.

ROD AND REEL

Fishing for whiting is made more pleasurable if we use a light outfit rather than old-fashioned heavy 'stick-and-crank' tackle. Certainly when the tide isn't running so hard we can often get away with using a small lead to hold the gear down. You can also get away with using a light spinning rod and fixed-spool reel.

PREPARING A WHITING FOR BAIT

Cut a fillet off the fish using a sharp knife.

Slice the fillet in half lengthways.

Now cut the fillet lengthways into 1cm to 2cm strips.

Pass the hook, which must be very sharp, through the whiting strip.

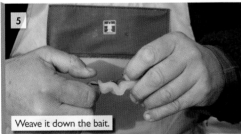
Weave it down the bait.

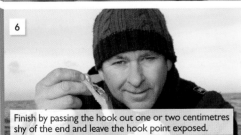
Finish by passing the hook out one or two centimetres shy of the end and leave the hook point exposed.

TOP TIPS

Soft Tip: Using a soft-tipped rod will help to increase your hook-up rate when fishing for smaller fish. The flexibility in the tip will clearly show the difference between when a fish is just plucking at the bait and when it has taken the bait properly. A hooked fish will give a much more pronounced bend in the soft tip.

Attracting Fish: Whiting are shoal fish that feed and hunt together. The shoals often consist of hundreds or thousands of fish that are competing with each other. We can use this to help us to catch more by simply using two-hook or three-hook traces, and leaving the first hooked fish for a while longer on the bottom. This fish's efforts to escape will attract the other fish to the remaining baits, resulting in double or treble hook-ups.

Fluorocarbon: Whiting have a habit of ruining traces because they twist and turn so much. Very often the traces get tangles in them. Using fluorocarbon hooklength line can help prevent this damage because it's so much stiffer than standard monofilament.

Waste Not, Want Not: The remaining head and guts from the filleted whiting can be a super-effective bait for the much larger cod and bass. This is a much underused bait that often produces huge fish!

Keep It Fresh: Because a piece of fresh whiting is so tough it will last a lot longer on the hook than a piece of thawed-out bait. But it's still important to change it regularly because the scent soon gets washed out. A fresh bait very often produces an instant response.

Alluring: Sometimes if the fish are being a little bit reluctant, savage bites can be encouraged with just a small movement to the bait by a gentle lift up and then back down again. This extra movement seems to provoke an attack from the fish.

A soft-tipped rod will clearly show when a whiting has struck.

much nodding constantly, now is the time to lift the rod and start reeling – not striking, just reel and keep on reeling. You will begin to feel some serious weight as you reel into the fish and, if you do feel it, just keep reeling and slowly raise the rod tip high, reeling all the time; this will set the hook properly.

SHOCK ABSORBER

DON'T drop the rod tip – keep it as high as you can, because you will then feel the fish fighting back and it will start bucking and shaking its head hard. The raised rod will absorb all of this and will react by bouncing in response; this is the satisfying bounce of a hooked big cod that skippers love to see and anglers love to feel!

PLAY THE GAME…

Playing the fish to the boat is a simple matter of keeping constant and steady pressure – a smooth action by reeling in line when you can and allowing the big fish to bounce and take line when it wants to. Slowly and surely the cod will come nearer and nearer; it will tire as it nears the boat and is normally well beaten by the time it's netted. Congratulations on your first 20-pounder!

TOP TIP

Although the cod appears to be well on the road to recovery, it doesn't mean that you should keep every one you catch. Simply keep only what you need and return the rest. Us recreational sea anglers should do all WE can to help conserve our fish stocks – and every little bit counts!

A big cod always brings a smile to the face!

You'll need big hooks in tandem to snare a big cod.

When you feel a bite, let out line to be sure the fish has taken the bait.

HOW TO TROT THE BAIT BACK AND LOCATE BIG COD

RAISE THE TRACE A FEW FEET AND LOWER AGAIN. REPEAT THIS UNTIL YOU FIND THE FISH

THE BETTER COD ARE FURTHER DOWNTIDE

LOWER THE TRACE TO THE BOTTOM

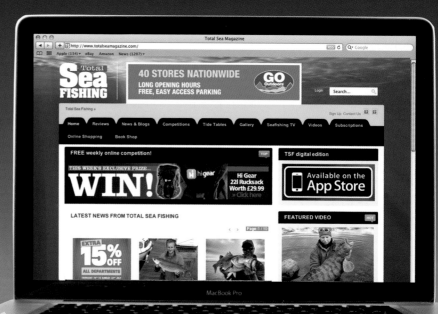

The Lure Of
BASS

Keep costs down as **Jim O'Donnell** explains how you can target bass for less than £2 per session!

There's a belief that modern lure fishing is expensive, but when you weigh up the cost of shore fishing baits like lug, rag, squid and peeler, just how much gets chucked in the sea at the end of a session? Balance the bite per pound of bait to one £15 lure that can be used to catch an infinite number of fish and you'll find that lure fishing is actually very cheap!

In the past 10 months I've fished 41 sessions but only lost about £75 worth of lures and line – that works out at just £1.83 per trip!

This bass fell for one of my favourite lures – a Megabass X-120 SW.

ADDICTIVE FISHING!

This type of lure fishing is addictive and has to be the most exciting way to fish. You travel light and actually go and find the fish rather than sitting waiting for one to find your bait.

You start working your lure in a likely looking spot and suddenly you feel a thump as a bass grabs your lure – it's like being plugged into mains electricity! The rod slams over as the fish runs for cover and line melts off the spool, you're suddenly pumped full of adrenaline and your hands and legs shake as you try to gain control of the fish. Once you've got the upper hand, you guide the fish through the rocks to the net or fish grip and lift it from the water. You're still shaking as you pose for a photograph and you have a permanent grin on your face – that's the magic of lure fishing!

It really is so simple, that's why it's the fastest-growing aspect of sea fishing – all you need is a rod and reel, a box with a dozen plugs and a couple of tools. I prefer to wear a fishing waistcoat in which I can store my box of lures, a pair of pliers for

unhooking and a fish grip for landing fish. This kit is so versatile that you can use it from a beach, rocks or a boat; the same gear will cover all these without you having to buy more specialised rods and reels.

I've found it best to use a front-drag fixed-spool reel as you can preset the drag to give line when a bass hits. One of the problems with rear-drag reels is that you can accidentally knock the rear knob and back it off – that's the last thing you want when you're casting with braid! If your drag is too loose, the spool will spin as you're casting and the thin braid will cut into your finger like a cheese wire. If you've ever had a braid cut you'll know what I mean!

The pictures here are some taken on a trip to Cork Harbour, in Ireland, where I fished with local guide Richie Ryan of 'Eire Bass' aboard his purpose-built bass boat. Richie specialises in surface fishing for bass and, as the images show, he's good at it as we had great sport with several fish to 6lb.

If you've never tried modern lure fishing, check out my guide to help you select the correct kit, then go out and enjoy the most addictive form of fishing!

MY MUST-HAVE LURE

The Megabass X-120 SW has to be one of my favourite lures of the last few years! It's the smaller brother of the Megabass X-140 SW and because of its slender profile it's a perfect sandeel imitation. The X-120 is a shallow-swimming floating plug; you cast and retrieve it with the odd twitch of the rod tip and it'll roll and wiggle, side to side, just like a natural sandeel. The X-120 SW features a lightweight internal tungsten weight transfer system to aid casting and is the perfect lure for calm, clear-water conditions on shallow beaches, in estuaries or over shallow kelp beds. I've had more takes on this lure than any other lure this year so it's definitely one to keep in the top of the box.
Length 120mm, weight 12.5g, with Owner ST-46 treble hooks.
Available from *www.basslures.co.uk*

Norway
Nature Travel

DinTur

THE BEST SHORE FISHING AREAS IN NORWAY!

Explore Norway's breathtaking coastline and let our local guides introduce you to the fishing holiday of a lifetime. We have 'selected' centres for shore fishing, with tried and tested marks ready for you to fish. Target huge cod, halibut and wolfish, along with the specimen sized pollack, plaice and dabs, on the light tackle.

- **BREATHTAKING COASTLINE**
- **THREE HOT SPOT LOCATIONS**

SPECTACULAR SHORE & BOAT FISHING HOLIDAYS
EXPERIENCE THE BEST SEA FISHING IN EUROPE!

EXTRAORDINARY FISHING FROM THE BOAT!

From the southernmost parts to far above the Arctic Circle, Norway's seas offer year-round fishing for a huge variety of species that can be caught from boat or from the shore. Din Tur holidays combine the very best accommodation and boats with the most outstanding sea fishing locations in the whole of Norway.

- **SELF-DRIVE BOAT FISHING**
- **CHARTER BOAT FISHING**

BOOK NOW FOR 2013 & 2014

FISHING HOLIDAYS IN NORWAY

Visit our NEW website to find out more and book your holiday **www.dintur.co.uk**

Contact: **Ian Peacock** • Email: **peacock@dintur.co.uk** • Tel: **01914 472 363** • Mob: **07763576995**

SCAN THE QR CODE TO VIEW OUR WEBSITE

Spring Into
ACTION

Roger Mortimore joined England international **Dave Chidzoy** as he revealed his top tips and secrets on spring plaice fishing.

As the sea temperature rises after the winter, one of the first spring species to arrive inshore is the plaice. And plaice make perfect targets from late March to early April because that's when they venture nearer Britain's coastline to feed, having spent all of the cold snap spawning in deep water.

One man who really knows how to coax these fantastic flatties onto the hook is shore ace Dave Chidzoy, and he certainly lived up to his reputation when I joined him on his local Chesil Beach in Dorset to get some hot tips on the best rigs and baits. The conditions couldn't have been better, with a warm, light wind, a calm sea and a mid-range tide – all ideal elements for plaice.

Apart from match fishing at top level, Dave loves pleasure fishing and targeting a particular species at different times of the year helps to hone his skills.

Dave shared some of his tips: "Good bait is the key and worm is the top bait for plaice so I give them a choice of fresh blow lug, rag and frozen black lug. That way I'll find out what they prefer on the day.

"I also always use two rods. One will be banged out to a maximum range of around 150 yards because that's where the worm beds are located on this particular stretch, while the other will hit the 80yd to 100yd mark to find a gulley where the plaice may be. The moment I've found where the fish are feeding, I'll fish both rods at that distance."

His theory produced instant results as a dogfish and a dab fell to the rod at shorter range. They weren't the species

we were after but showed that his bait and rig choice were working. But when he wound in the second rod he could feel the weight of a decent fish that put up a good scrap in the backwash. After a final flurry, Dave slid a cracking plaice up the beach, its light brown back covered with bright orange spots. It took the scales down to just over 2lb – not bad for a first cast on his long-distance rod with the shorter range producing the dab.

At long range Dave said he could feel his lead dragging through ridges of mud or clay; this is obviously where the worms were buried and the plaice were feeding so that's where he'd put both his rigs.

The next cast produced a small female dragonet, which, according to Dave, is a great sign. He said: "If you start catching these you know you're on the right ground. Whenever I've caught them in the past I've always taken plaice soon afterwards."

> *After a final flurry, Dave slid a cracking plaice up the beach, its light brown back covered with orange spots.*

TACTICS

As we waited for the next bite he showed me some of his rigs and explained how and why they work so well.

His preferred rig is a three-hook clipped-down rig with snoods 12 to 18 inches long armed with size 2 Aberdeen hooks. He adds a small floating bead to the top or middle snood to help

lift the bait off the bottom. This extra movement helps to attract the plaice that find their food by sight and scent. The coloured beads are used for sight and the worms give off the scent so you've got both avenues covered.

When the current is running hard Dave uses Namix or Breakaway leads to hold bottom. These will either hold the baits static or slowly drag downtide covering ground to find the fish. When the current dies down to a trickle he'll change to a plain lead and cast it well uptide of his position and let the current drag it downtide. This tactic covers a lot of ground and is a sure way to find a plaice or two. Like many other species, plaice feed best when there's current to either carry food to them or they use it to cover ground without wasting energy swimming.

Our conversation was interrupted when Dave noticed that the tip of one of his rods had straightened then pulled down into a curve again. When it lifted for a second time he said: "I reckon that's another fish. Sometimes you get the classic nodding on the rod tip when they attack the bait but on other occasions just the extra weight of the fish on the rig is enough to move the lead a little. You have to be aware of these subtle bites."

I could see the bend in his rod tip as he reeled in and, sure enough, another plaice hit the shingle. This one was only 1lb 8oz but it was still the target fish and backed up his theory – if you catch a dragonet, the plaice aren't far away. Another tip Dave gave me regarding bites was never to strike when you see a bite. Flatfish are slow feeders so need

Dave's first long-range cast produced this fine 2lb plaice.

A dab and a plaice – can you 'spot' the difference...

plenty of time to swallow the bait before you even think of reeling in.

The area we were fishing was well away from the more convenient spots straight in front of a car park. The whole stretch of beach looked the same to me but Dave explained the reasons for his choice of location, saying: "It's down to fishing this area for many years. Although Chesil looks like a long, featureless stretch of shingle, the sea bed in some areas is made up of features that hold the fish. There's a patch of mud in front of us here but 100 to 200 yards left or right it's just gravel and sand.

"The mud is also home to worms, shrimps and small crabs, which various species of fish home in on. They're happy to linger around these stretches of mud for long periods searching out their favourite food."

PRIME TIME

As it neared low water the bites stopped, but Dave was sure that the prime time was yet to come, when the current increases on the flood and light starts to fade. During the slack period he put spare rigs back in

the rig wallet and just had two spare rigs ready to go – one for each rod – explaining that there would be less to find and pack away in the dark. Looking up at his rod tips we could see a good bend in them, meaning that the current was running and it was time to see if this really was the 'prime time' for plaice. Dave wound

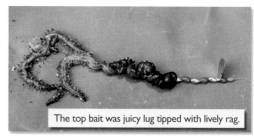

The top bait was juicy lug tipped with lively rag.

Dragonets are a sign that you're fishing the right ground for plaice.

> *As the fish got closer, the rod was still bending, and when it reached the backwash Dave was forced to stop winding.*

in both rods and cast fresh baits out, saying: "This increase in current combined with fading light is when plaice often feed best, just before they get their heads down for the night." The fresh bait obviously did the trick as the tip of his right-hand rod bent over then straightened. Dave jumped up to keep a close eye on the rod and could see the line slowly moving downtide. Once he was certain that the fish was on, he picked up the rod and started winding.

As the fish got closer, the rod was still bending, and when it reached the backwash Dave was forced to stop winding as it swam to the left.

We both knew that Dave was into a decent-sized fish but the huge brown

shape that emerged from the water and onto the beach as he gave one final lift left the pair of us speechless. Flapping on the shingle was the biggest shore-caught plaice I have ever seen.

The fish was a cracker at 3lb 12oz – a mere 10oz short of Dave's personal best. In days gone by this specimen would have been viewed as a fish capable of providing the ultimate fish supper, but Dave's priority is conservation.

The fish was kept out of the water for the minimum amount of time for weighing and photographing before being gently released back into the sea.

Dave explained: "Fish of this size are prime breeding stock and always need to be returned. She will be capable of laying a vast amount of eggs to ensure we have more fish for the future. It's the way forward and the satisfaction of seeing a fish like that swim away is far more rewarding then seeing it on a plate surrounded by some chips and peas."

The big plaice and Dave's wise words made a fitting end to a superb eye-opening session. Although I've been fishing for more than 50 years, spending time with Dave made me realise that you never stop learning – especially if you're in the company of someone who has mastered the sport.

TOP TIPS

1 Always take a good supply of fresh lug and rag with frozen black lug as an alternative.

2 Try a plain lead as the tide eases and let the current slowly drag it along to find fish.

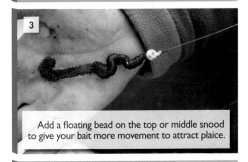

3 Add a floating bead on the top or middle snood to give your bait more movement to attract plaice.

4 When you're fishing for plaice, never strike a bite when you first see it. Let the fish take the bait for at least two or three minutes before you reel in.

Spring plaice are hungry – this one has taken the bait and the beads.

PLAICE FACTS

1 The British Shore Record is a monster of 8lb 6oz 14dr, caught on Southbourne Beach, Dorset, by R Moore back in 1989. The British Boat Record weighed 10lb 3oz 8dr and was caught by 16-year-old H Gardiner in Longa Sound, Scotland.

2 The plaice's habitat extends from The Barents Sea to the north, down to the Mediterranean Sea to the south.

3 Plaice are fairly slow growing and if they avoid capture they may live for more than 40 years.

4 They prefer to live over a sea bed made up of sand, mud and gravel. They have a particular liking for mussel beds but can sometimes be seen 'sunbathing' high up on reefs.

Dave's prediction that the flood tide at dusk would be 'prime time' was spot on, with this superb 3lb 12oz plaice being the proof.

Barking
MAD!

Smoothhounds fight hard and can run circles around you, leaving you aching, bruised but in total ecstasy.

This is a starry hound – it can be identified by the white star-like spots on its body.

GET MORE FROM YOUR TABLET

Total Sea FISHING

STICK SOMETHING AWESOME ON IT

Total Sea Fishing is available on single, six and 12-issue subscriptions

WORKS ON SMARTPHONES TOO!

powered by

MagazineCloner.com
Whitelabel Digital Publishing Solutions

Visit iTunes or the Android Market and search 'Total Sea Fishing' to download the app.
Once that is installed you can purchase the magazine from those stores or at www.pocketmags.com

PLUS! These great fishing titles are also available

Summer Bass
BASICS

Top boat angler and charter skipper **Glen Milligan**
explains the fundamentals for the best success with bass…

If you get it right, you too can catch a magnificent fish like this!

Of all the fish that we see and catch each season, I'm sure that the bass is the favourite! Every now and then we get one turn up as a by-catch to a lucky angler; that happens probably one trip in three and, if you're really lucky, it will be a sizeable specimen big enough for the table.

These fish not only look truly stunning with their gleaming silver flanks, but also taste superb! The biggest bass caught on board my boat *Wight Huntress* last year weighed in at a whopping 12lb! Again, this fish was caught accidentally while we were anchored fishing for blonde rays.

PROTECTION…

Sea bass is a regular feature on menus in many top restaurants throughout the country, and for good reason. It's in high demand due to its superb flavour. This, unfortunately, has led to it being overfished, which has obviously resulted in a decline in its numbers! This is even more worrying because the species has a particularly slow growth rate. Its popularity has been its near downfall – therefore the bass needs to be protected!

Various measures have been taken to try to protect the future of the bass, one of which was the creation of many inshore bass nursery areas (no-take zones.) There's plenty of controversy over these protection areas but, one thing's for sure, the inshore areas and harbours around the south coast are now brimming with small bass! It's hoped that these small ones will grow on and move

offshore – returning as spawning fish at a later date.

So, as it is now, I believe that we have a 'decent' bass population – there are certainly enough fish for us to specifically target them sensibly.

HUNGRY BEASTS

The bass is an aggressive creature – it's an out-and-out attacker, a predator that often hunts its prey in packs. Like most fish, it can pass long periods of time without feeding – but when it does it will feed ravenously, often engulfing large fish such as pouting, whiting and mackerel. Take a look at the mouth of a bass; it opens to form a huge cavern capable of taking in prey fish half its size!

POPULAR

As the bass is such a popular species, it follows that there are charter trips made specifically to target them. The idea of jumping on a boat and bagging up on these silver beauties can be very appealing. The reality, though, can sometimes be far removed, because targeting them can often be as frustrating as it can be exhilarating.

It must be understood from the outset that, similar to wreck fishing, there can often be plenty of time taken up travelling both to and from the speciality bass marks and between them. A common problem is that if the bass don't want to feed, then they simply won't! And, when they do turn on to feed, it's often when the tide is ripping through, making drifts short and fishing difficult,

particularly over rough, snaggy ground! If the bass was easy to catch then maybe it wouldn't be held in such high esteem. I am convinced that it's the sporting qualities, mystery and taste that draw anglers to the bass.

THE CHARTER

As a charter skipper I'm looking to do more and more bass trips. I just love these truly majestic fish – beautiful silver with spines and razors; true stunners! I love catching them and I love the excitement of the drift, waiting for a hit! I get even more excited when I discover, or hear of, new marks and a possible untapped bounty, and then there's the reward of finding them and watching customers get one in the net – the look of elation on a customer's face when the plan succeeds is second to none.

It's exciting during these times. And, if you're a boat owner, you too can experience this and the wonders of modern-day bass angling.

> "The bass is an aggressive creature – it's an out-and-out attacker, a predator that often hunts its prey in packs."

ON YOUR MARKS…

I like to visit 'old favourite' marks, where I feel confident that my customers will catch. I work my boat out of Langstone Harbour, near Portsmouth, and one such area is a couple of banks 20 miles

A rotten-bottom is a good idea when over reefs – telephone wire is ideal.

The Portland rig is Glen's only choice for bassing.

Lures, such as these blue-and-white Red Gill Evolution sandeels, are perfect for targeting bass.

Live sandeels are deadly, especially for the smaller bass.

offshore where the ground isn't too snaggy but, as is typical of any bass mark, it's in an area of strong tide and more than 100 feet of water. At marks like this, the best way to target bass is with livebaits such as sandeels, pout and mackerel, or with lures such as shads and Red Gills.

RIG
Whatever method is chosen, the lure or bait is presented on the same trace, the 'Portland rig'.

This rig has evolved over the years and is indeed very popular and widely used for bassing. In fact, as it works so well, I see no need to use anything else. As can be seen from the diagram (overleaf), the rig is essentially a flowing trace mounted on a short vertical monofilament spine. As it's designed to prevent tangles and also to present the bait as naturally as possible, I have no hesitation in recommending this approach for charter anglers.

RODS
For rod choice I like to use something soft with plenty of action; a 6lb to 12lb-class rod is ideal as we are only using light leads and a rod in this class will really enhance the fight of this true sportfish!

REELS
I like to use a medium-sized fixed-spool reel, quite simply because it is faster for getting the gear down and faster on the retrieve. This can be important because quite often we need to get that rig straight down into the catch zone, with no messing about.

A fast retrieve is essential because these fish are true fighters – not only will they try to swim away; they will also swim straight up and at you! More of that later, but what is relevant here is that a fast retrieve will help you keep up with the fish, stopping it from shedding your hook! Load the reel with 30lb braid, 20 feet of 20lb leader and you're ideally set up!

LEADS
The lead size is a key element here. You need to be using one that's light enough to present the rig naturally as well as being able to feel the bottom – this is so important. You need to

TIDE FLOW

TAKE ZONE

HOW TO DRIFT FOR BASS

BASS WILL MOST LIKELY BE WAITING ON THE DOWNTIDE EDGE

RUNNING LINE

SWIVEL

BEAD

SWIVEL

BEAD

20 INCHES
OF 40LB
MONO LINE

6 FEET OF 20LB
FLUOROCARBON

SWIVEL

TELEPHONE WIRE

LURE

LEAD

A light boat rod coupled with a fixed-spool reel will enhance your sport.

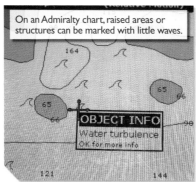

On an Admiralty chart, raised areas or structures can be marked with little waves.

know that you have touched bottom when you lower down, and you need to know exactly where you are during the drift. This is so you will know to reel up as you go up the bank, then let line out as you go down the other side.

CATCH MY DRIFT

As with any drift fishing situation, the skipper will line up the boat for the pass, then describe the drift to the anglers as it goes along. This is important, because the bass will often be found in the same area on the bank and the skipper should tell you where you are at all times for the best chance of success.

As you approach a new mark, I guarantee that you'll be bristling with anticipation over a few details, such as: what will the mark look like

on the sounder, will there be any other boats there, will there be any fish and will you catch them? This, of course, is all exciting stuff!

I can recall one trip when, on approaching the mark, I noticed two things straightaway. Firstly, there was another boat already fishing. But this wasn't just any boat; it was a commercial fisherman using rod-and-line tactics for bass.

Although initially a shocker, this was, in fact, a very good sign, because it meant that he wouldn't be wasting his time there if there were no fish, which made me feel more confident that there could be a good head of fish about.

Secondly, I noticed another great sign – there was a clearly visible boil created by the tide hitting the bank and squeezing the water over the top; this, in turn, disrupts and confuses any baitfish, making them easy prey for the waiting bass. This boil is referred to nautically as an 'area of overfalls'. These areas are easy to find, because they're clearly marked on charts due to the danger they hold for smaller vessels that can be knocked around in the rough water.

All was looking good, although I felt that I should have been at the mark a couple of hours earlier and at the beginning of the tide, which can often be prime time. Although we arrived during the middle of the tide, things still worked out very well and we all had bass, some of which were touching double figures. This just goes to prove that the theory outlined here is spot on and, if you pay attention to all the little details and get yourself involved, you too can enjoy the same buzz that I get from bassing.

Daylight
RUBBERY

Lure fishing experts **Nathan Taylor** and **Nick Bennett** have adopted SAS tactics in a bid to win more battles with specimen bass, wrasse and pollack. **Roger Mortimore** explains…

The dynamic duo of Nathan Taylor and Nick Bennett have armed themselves with the sort of vessels favoured by special forces around the world so that they can reach vast areas of virgin coastline that normal fishing boats are unable to reach.

The pair, who run Cornish-based Lure Masters, have invested in two RHIBs (rigid hulled inflatable boats), which are capable of entering areas a mere 30 centimetres deep. And they can reach these untapped marks in ultra-quick time thanks to their power-packed engines. So when the call came inviting me to have a go at fishing from these novel boats while using the ultimate in sporting tactics – soft-plastic and latex lures on light tackle – the car was packed before the receiver had time to cool down.

Lure Masters has evolved from Bass Masters and expanded its business to target fish not just from the shore – which can be a little limiting – but also afloat as the guys continue developing new techniques using soft lures with amazing results.

As Nathan explained: "We're getting into areas no other boat can manage and these marks are also impossible to reach on foot so the fish at them have never seen an angler. It really is exploring new ground.

"We're using really light gear and fishing soft lures right into the kelp and gullies where wrasse up to 5lb are lurking and will suddenly dart out and slam into the lures. It's real heart-stopping stuff."

On the drive down the M5, images of rod-buckling wrasse putting my gossamer gear to the test kept flashing through my mind and I also felt it would be an opportunity to practise tactics with some specialist lures from the Mr Fish brand.

I certainly wasn't disappointed when I saw the vessels being used for our expedition. Nathan's RHIB is a heavy-duty 3.8m X Pro powered by a 15hp Tohatsu outboard. With the engine leg lifted she floats in just 30 centimetres of water. Nathan also carries a fishfinder, VHF radio, walkie-talkie and life vests. Nick runs a Zodiac 5.5m RHIB powered by a 100hp Evinrude outboard and is fully equipped with a Garmin fishfinder/depth sounder, VHF radio, walkie-talkie, flares, anchor and self-inflating life vests. The beauty of these boats is that they can be launched from the trickiest shore marks and can then be manoeuvred into spots normally reserved for kayaks.

Our opening trip was from Challaborough Beach in Devon where I joined Nick and Nathan along with fellow guide Matt Arnold for a high-speed trip out to the Eddystone Reef. The weather conditions were perfect – a flat-calm sea with hardly a cloud in the sky and as wrasse feed mainly during daylight, the scene was set for some bumper sport.

Apart from the prospects of some exciting fishing, a 30-knot ride in a RHIB is quite exhilarating and gets you on the mark very quickly!

The Eddystone is one of the country's most notorious reefs, situated 14 miles south/southeast of Plymouth. The treacherous rocks have been a graveyard for many ships and sailors.

It's also home to specimen pollack, bass and several other species, but there is one downside to the famous mark… divers.

They can hinder a good drift and on one of the few times we managed to get into the zone for a short period, Nick hooked a pollack of 3lb that took a flier rigged above a Savage Gear Sandeel.

Another drift produced some huge launce and a couple of herring but with access to the drifts almost impossible due to the divers, we decided to head in to attack the inshore waters.

Nick groaned, saying: "The divers can be a pain on some of the marks we fish; obviously the wrecks and reefs hold the fish that we're after. Those features are also of interest to divers and with the clear water we have down here, the numbers of divers seems to be growing every year."

RESCUE DRAMA

As we sped in we heard a call from the Brixham coastguard requesting assistance for a 20ft vessel with engine failure five miles east of the Eddystone. Our location was two to three miles northeast of the reef so Nick responded and offered to locate the vessel and stand by until help arrived. Once we'd located the vessel, Nick informed the coastguard of our position, when another call came over the radio from a larger craft that was en route to tow the stricken vessel back to Plymouth. To while away the time a few strings of feathers were produced and we soon had a couple of dozen mackerel on board, which would be destined for the barbecue that evening!

A new personal best wrasse of 4lb 8oz for Roger on a soft-plastic lure.

Nathan Taylor applies side strain to prevent a wrasse from getting its head into the kelp.

Once the stricken vessel was safely under tow back to Plymouth, we headed to our next location – close inshore in Bigbury Bay. We may have lost some planned fishing time but it was satisfying doing our bit for the coastguards.

THE ACTION STARTS WITH A BANG!

Nick skilfully nosed the RHIB between some shallow reefs and we cast our lures into the crystal-clear waters. Just as my lure hit the water, Nathan's rod slammed over and line was ripped from the reel at speed. The fish went to ground in the kelp so Nick had to fire up the engine and ease the boat into position, meaning that Nathan had a vertical pull to free the fish. Once he'd heaved it away from the underwater snags, a beautifully marked 5lb-plus ballan wrasse was safely in the net. More action followed, with small pollack and wrasse of various sizes hitting the lures and, believe me, there's nothing subtle about the take from a wrasse! Anyone who hasn't tried this form of fishing needs to put it on their bucket list.

There you are, gently bouncing the lure on the bottom, when a dark shape darts from the weed, grabs the lure and rushes back into cover. You have to give them serious stick to try to slow them down; spinning rods are bent double and the sight can be quite hilarious, especially when there's a double hook-up. Matt wrapped the day up with a feisty 4lb ballan wrasse that took a 16cm Savage Gear Sandeel before we headed in for the mackerel barbecue.

Back at base we were treated to a banquet that Nick's wife, Lisa, had prepared for us: barbecued topside of beef, her special fisherman's veg-bake, salad and rice and those delicious mackerel washed down with a cold beer – the perfect end to a perfect day!

DAY TWO WAS EVEN BETTER!

The following day we decided to concentrate on the inshore reefs to the east of Challaborough. Nathan and Matt headed out first while Nick and I were joined by Nick's six-year-old son Charlie, who was dying to get into action.

As we rounded Burgh Island –

Nathan and the wrasse both grin for the camera!

there's an exclusive hotel there where rooms cost a small fortune and Agatha Christie is among the famous names to have signed the register – there was certainly no mystery about what the day might bring. The moment we saw Nathan's and Matt's rods bent double, we knew there would be plenty of action on the menu.

As Nick eased the throttle down, all we could

Nick displays a 3lb pollack, just one of the many species that hit the lures.

hear was manic laughter as both rods were doubled over before Nathan slid the net under a brace of pollack. They were only 3lb and 4lb but brilliant fun on the light gear.

My gear was a US-style 6ft Ugly Stik matched with a tiny Abu Revo baitcasting reel loaded with 20lb braid topped with three feet of 20lb fluorocarbon. This would extract maximum sport from our main target – ballan wrasse.

To start with I thought I'd try a Reins Ring Claw, a dark-brown soft latex lure, as Mick Ward has found that dark colours seem to produce more takes. With it rigged on a 15g jighead, I dropped it over the side and jigged it once before my rod tip was slammed over – yes Mick, they do like dark colours!

All I could do was hang on and try to keep it out of the kelp; the drag was set so it would only just give line but the crash-diving wrasse still ripped a few yards off. It went 4lb 8oz on the scales, a new personal best on a lure and what an amazing scrap!

As we drifted around this small reef we found fish everywhere, so many that we lost count after a dozen. It's so close inshore that I guess most boats pass it by on their way to deeper water, thus missing out on some crazy sport.

After two hours of hectic action, Nick

Nathan's sleeve says it all – a double hook-up produced a few moments of madness!

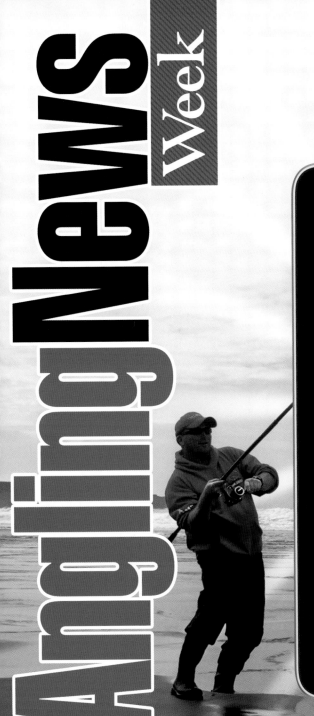

JUST TAKE

Help Stop Litter Spoiling Our Beaches And Coastline

As anglers we know we have a responsibility to protect wildlife and our sport's reputation by leaving the coast free of angling-related litter – but let's not stop there…

Next time you are fishing **just take 5** minutes to pick up someone else's litter or pick up **5 items** of litter to dispose of.

Never forget, the public's opinion of us as sportsmen and women depends on us leaving only footprints behind.

ANGLING TRUST

THE VOICE OF ANGLING

Join Us Today: 0844 770 0616

www.anglingtrust.net

The Just Take 5 initiative was created by the Angling Trust's Wyvern Marine Region and is supported by the Marine Conservation Society

SAVE UP TO 69%* ON THIS TOP ANGLING MAGAZINE

ON SALE SECOND FRIDAY EVERY MONTH.

>> Total Sea Fishing magazine is written by experts with a die-hard passion for the sport. Their aim is to you help you improve your skills and become a more effective angler – be it boat, shore or bass fishing. It is informative, helpful, honest, and trusted by thousands.

Each month you'll find no-holds-barred reviews of the latest tackle, detailed step-by-step features on how to catch the fish you seek, several pages dedicated to your catch reports plus a section focusing entirely on boat fishing.

WIN A SUPERB HOLIDAY FOR FOUR WORTH £1,200!

BAG YOUR BEST COD EVER! Glen Milligan's tips on targeting the big fish

REVEALED! Top-secret species mark at Barry Docks

BE A GREAT ANGLER Roger Mortimore's advice turns novices into experts

Sea Academy
• Tie better knots
• Understand the weather
• Build great rigs

Blonde Bombshell
Neil Bryant targets big rays

INCORPORATING TOTAL BOAT FISHING

Where Anglers
DARE

Shetland marks the northern extremity of the British Isles
and defines the final 'truly unexplored' frontier for UK sea anglers.
Steve Souter explored the magical location with incredible results.

Shetland's Jeemie Reid caught this 29lb monster coalfish on a huge Red Gill lure.

Despite fantastic stories of unbelievable fishing and invitations stretching back many years, I had never managed to drag my carcass across the sea to Shetland. That all changed recently, though, and I experienced the most incredible fishing of my life. The average size of fish was ridiculously large, and the sheer weight of numbers finally collapsed me to my haunches in an exhausted but utterly satisfied stupor.

THE SHETLANDS

Located some 400 miles south of the Arctic Circle, and plumb between Scotland and Norway, the Shetlands are a jigsaw-like archipelago of more than 100 island and mini islets. Getting there was no great trial and I drove off the North Link ferry into Lerwick full of anticipation. My regular fishing partner, Scott Gibson, and I were met by Shetland trio Laurence Williamson, Mark Duncan and Jeemie Reid… all of whom are obsessive sea anglers with intimate connections to the fishing industry, which, along with oil, is the economic lifeblood of these alluring islands.

A little over an hour later we were leaving the quay at Cullinvoe, blasting a trail past beautifully stark coastal edges towards the outer extremity of the British Isles. Licensed boats in one form or another are dotted all around the Shetland Isles, but there are no full-time angling charter boats as such in the immediate vicinity. Laurence, however, had worked a masterstroke in enlisting the aid of two friendly and knowledgeable boat crews to take us out to the fish. Indeed, this was to be a two-boat assault, with Scott and Mark joined by local lad Stuart Bruce on the 27ft *Mareel*, jointly skippered by brothers Owen and Raymond Strachan. I pitched in with Laurence and Jeemie aboard the 26ft *Joanne Claire*, run by Ian Nicolson and Richard Gray.

GATHER THE WINDS

The biggest problem with plotting a boat fishing adventure to anywhere on Shetland is the huge risk of spoiling weather. The area isn't like Norway, or some other cold northern cloister, where safe shelter can be found by slinking up a convenient high-sided fjord. Rather, it's a landscape laid bare to the full hellish fury of the north Atlantic Ocean on the one flank, and exposed to vicious assaults from the North Sea on the other. We were unbelievably fortunate in the wind stakes and hardly a ripple and only the gentlest of lazy swells confronted us.

Our destination was Muckle Flugga located just north of the island of Unst and some 30 minutes away. Often tagged the northernmost point of the British Isles, geographical sticklers would point out that a smaller neighbouring rock, Out Stack, is the rightful laird of that lofty honour. Local folklore has it that Flugga and Out Stack were the result of two love-drunk giants tossing great rocks at each other as they vied for the attention of a beautiful mermaid. The tale concludes that the same devilish half-woman did a fine job of later drowning them both!

Flugga lighthouse sits like a portentous, big, white albatross atop perhaps the most inhospitable nest of stone that I have ever seen. Steeply sloping rocks then plunge dramatically downwards, rending the sea and serving warning to the foolhardy to maintain a safe distance. The scene of many an old shipwreck, and a place of ghosts if you ask me, there's a palpable goose-bump atmosphere of lingering suspense born of strong visual first impressions, a little fear perhaps and the sound of a thousand high-pitched seabird voices. Thankfully we wouldn't be courting catastrophe by venturing too close.

TITANIC TACKLE

The favourite rod among the crews was the Team Daiwa TDXB3050, while battle-scarred 6/0 Penn Senators carrying at least 80lb braids were the dominant reels. Rigs were quickly knocked up on the way out to the fishing grounds. Laurence's rigs were simple blood loops tied in 100lb to 150lb mono to 12/0 Norwegian eels – or Gummi Makks to give them their correct name. These were simply looped into place through the swivel on the lure. Either a bar pirk of up to 1½lb with the treble hook removed, or a similarly heavy lead is attached to the bottom. I don't usually fish this big or as heavy but, following Laurence's lead, I made a couple of these basic three-hook rigs in 100lb mono with 10/0 Gummis, which were the biggest I possessed!

Our boat arrived first and Ian cut the Cygnus engine to begin the drift about a quarter of a mile off Flugga. Ian confirmed what I could see from peeping through the wheelhouse door at the sounder – a hard bottom and perfect cod country. He informed us that the depth would run out from 65 to 90 metres, but that the tide wasn't too strong as yet and we should enjoy a steady drift. Fearing instant snags, all of us left the fancy pirks in our boxes for now and clipped on plain 1¼lb Bopedo leads.

The depth wasn't killer and the leads were enough to keep the lines perpendicular. The method was no more complicated than a simple lift and drop back in classic pirking fashion. Cod to 14lb fell to Laurence and me, and a 10lb pollack went to Jeemie on the first pass over the rough ground. After a quick study of his plotter numbers, Ian repositioned the

Left to right: Scott Gibson, Owen Strachan, Raymond Strachan, Stuart Bruce and Mark Duncan (the Hairy Bear), show off a small selection of cracking fish.

The result of a good day's fishing – a spectacular 7lb-plus bar of silver!

gulley revealed, but low water also exposes the holes and gullies that can be targeted as the tide begins to flood and cover them over again.

Steve's fishing buddy for the night is local hot rod Tommy Wells, who has built up quite a reputation for himself as a quality angler. Wasting no time, Steve sets up his tackle and accurately casts a large peeler crab bait in the hole in a matter of minutes. He chooses to use crab and lug for this evening's session, because at this time of year there is no better bait for targeting bass, except for, possibly, a live pouting or sandeel.

Peeler crab is also the choice for Tommy, who also wastes no time in setting up, and with an equally accurate cast he has his bait in almost exactly the same spot as Steve. It is only a matter of moments before Tommy jumps up and grabs his rod.

"Hey Steve!" he exclaims, "I've

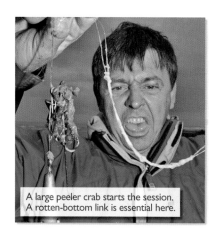

A large peeler crab starts the session. A rotten-bottom link is essential here.

got a fish on… it's scrapping well mate, it could even be the first bass of the night." But as the fish breaks the surface it becomes perfectly clear that this is no bass, because this 'scrappy' fish is, in fact, a slimy eel! Admittedly, it is a good fish which must weigh well over 2lb, but this is not the intended target species.

Tommy is first to catch with this 2lb eel.

An hour or so passes, and the tide is near to low water when Steve comments: "I am surprised that I have not had a bass yet, because the conditions are perfect.

"There is a slight roll on the sea, the air pressure is low and the timing is spot on! I just don't understand what's going on."

Then, as if by divine intervention, Steve's rod tip bounces a few times, which results in his line going slack.

He pounces on his rod and reels so that he can get in contact with the fish. He is expecting to feel some really good thumps after the slack is retrieved but, alas, all he feels is the knockings of a smaller fish and not the lunker he is hoping for.

Nevertheless, a fish is on and Steve hopes that at least it will be a little bass. But this fish does not feel like a bass and, as the fish surfaces, it is yet again clear that Steve has also been unlucky enough to hook an eel, which has completely destroyed his trace.

His rig is wrapped around the eel and

Steve sends the first offering on its way.

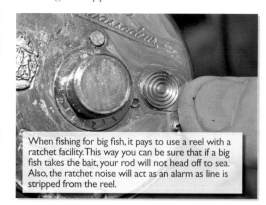

When fishing for big fish, it pays to use a reel with a ratchet facility. This way you can be sure that if a big fish takes the bait, your rod will not head off to sea. Also, the ratchet noise will act as an alarm as line is stripped from the reel.

Large lugworms are great bait for bass here.

BAITING UP

1 Squeeze the worm's guts upwards towards its head.

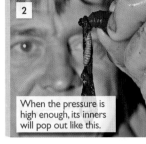

2 When the pressure is high enough, its inners will pop out like this.

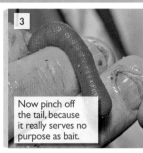

3 Now pinch off the tail, because it really serves no purpose as bait.

4 Thread one or two worms over the hook and up the snood.

5 Turn the snood around the top hook three or four times, then pass the hook through the worm as pictured.

6 Pull it all tight, and you should end up with a perfect bait like Steve's.

smothered in slime, rendering it useless. Reluctantly, Steve cuts the trace to release the eel, which he returns safely despite a few harsh words and ill wishes towards the pest!

Undeterred, Steve rigs up again, but this time he chooses to use lug instead of peeler crab. He feels that if the eels are on the feed, it is most likely that they will pick up any crab baits before a bass would.

He baits up with two large lug, which must surely tempt something different, and casts them into the hole. In just moments his rod tip rattles in a satisfying way to indicate

that this time a small bass must have taken the bait. The bite is a classic school bass bite, and Steve has no concerns in predicting that this is indeed the first bass of the trip. Sure enough, he is spot on and a bass of about 1lb reaches the secure hands of Steve. It is a perfect example of a good-quality and healthy fish, which he wastes no time in returning.

In true matchman style, Steve gets another lug bait in the sea within no time at all. He has not even had time to sit on his box when the rod tip rattles again to signify the presence of yet another school bass.

Steve's first fish is also an eel, but this one is a little smaller than Tommy's.

Steve kicks off the bass fishing with this beautiful little bar of silver.

This second fish turns out to be another great example of a healthy schoolie, which also weighs in at about the 1lb mark.

Now that Steve is sure the bass are beginning to show, he appears to step up into another gear and baits go into the water at a regular 10 to 15-minute basis. He ignores the peeler crab and stays with the lug baits, purely because he has no desire to become tangled up with another slimy eel, which, unless he is very lucky, will destroy the trace.

The tide is now well on its way in and much of the exposed ground is once again hidden by the sea. Steve decides that he will fish for about another hour or so, because he believes that soon the very best fishing time will have passed. Tommy is still steadily catching schoolies and eels, which he is having plenty of fun with. But he too knows that time is rapidly running out with regard to bagging a big fish.

Steve sends another perfectly prepared lug bait directly into the deep hole, which is becoming more of an effort to reach as the time rolls by. He sets his rod in the rest and stands back. It is possible to see the

Steve is sure that he has a very good fish on.

concentration and determination in his eyes as he watches the rod tip.

It is almost as if he is willing a good fish towards his bait.

Then, all of a sudden, all hell breaks loose as his rod literally leaps out of the rest, only to fall straight back into it as the line goes slack. "This has to be a good fish," says Steve. And, as he rapidly reels the slack back onto the reel, it is obvious that his statement is spot on, because no sooner has he made contact with the fish, than it starts to strip

line off the spool! "Bloody hell!" Steve exclaims. "This is a belter! I hope that the hooks are set properly because I want this one in!"

Steve scraps with the fish for a good five minutes before we get our first view of it. He could bully it in, but it is not worth the risk of losing it. Besides, he is also thoroughly enjoying a damn good tussle with the fish. The fish zips left and right as it enters the shallows in a desperate bid to regain its freedom. After all, how is this fish supposed to know that it will be returned unharmed? It is clear that this fish really is a cracker, and we are all trying to guess its weight, even before it is finally beached.

As Steve draws the fish expertly onto the beach, there can be no doubt that the bass must weigh at least 6lb or 7lb... possibly more!

In an attempt to return the fish as quickly as possible, we must take the pictures of this special capture as fast as we can. Both Steve and the fish warm to the cameras, and the job is done. But before we can say "nice one mate," Steve is on his way back to the water to return the fish.

Now that the bass have arrived, Steve steps up a gear and concentrates hard.

Steve is quite pleased with himself, as he kneels in the surf, allowing the magnificent fish to regain its strength. The real look of joy appears on his face, however, when the fish slowly saunters off into the surf and then, finally, with a flick of its tail, vanishes back into the depths.

This signifies the end of the session and Steve packs up his gear in the knowledge that he has once again produced the goods for the cameras. Yet again Mr Allmark has produced a very fine result, and this is all simply down to years of experience, dedication and local knowledge.

At last – payment for all of Steve's efforts. This cracker is at least 6lb!